Matthew Walsh guides the reader into a city full of stories with sex, graffiti, hurt, and the kind of humour that is both sprung from survival and makes you want to sit next to it at a party. *Terrarium* is a city-infused loneliness that is rooted in satire and surrealism. This book is so deeply queer that it should have its own brand.

> — CHARLIE PETCH, author of *Why I Was Late*

Terrarium is an exceptional collection of confessional poems. Each poem is a story that is so raw, powerful, and very emotional. I had chills reading these poems. This is one of my favourite poetry books ever.

> — HASAN NAMIR, author of *Umbilical Cord*

Matthew Walsh's *Terrarium* leaves me aching, inspired, in awe. To quote the poet themself, I am amazed at Walsh's power — "how much I have had to keep straight." This power manifests in Walsh's crafting of patient, artful meaning from the alienating flux of twenty-first century life and in their efforts to confront, resist, and counter the destructive limitations of straightness as a dominant cultural force. In performing this urgent, necessary work, *Terrarium* is as tender and attentive as it is transformative and profound.

> — DANIEL SCOTT TYSDAL, author of *The End Is in the Middle*

Also by Matthew Walsh

These are not the potatoes of my youth

MATTHEW WALSH
TERRARIUM

icehouse poetry

You had meant to move with a kind of largeness,
You had planned a heavy grace, an anguished dream.

— Gwendolyn MacEwen, "Dark Pines under Water"

CONTENTS

HEAD

Just ignore me
I am feeling better now
and removed my wisdom teeth
there was no other choice
in the mirror a face seeing
loss is reflected back at them
I thought *the mouth how it succumbs to little*
disintegrations you know
the world is full of found art
a pomegranate at Bathurst and Bloor
looks unreal outside the world
of fine art and myth
the red seeds usually symbolic
of the end of a unicorn hunt
to me the very fruity jawbone
of the produce aisle
What amazes me in life is frog power
the ability to regrow the self
with your own personal body
I'm sitting in a parkette with the head
of Gwendolyn MacEwen with remnants
of magnolia leaves
Imagine just wanting to spend life
writing everything down that you loved
about experience the myth and your reality
Just trying to remember my first time
reading the selected poems
but the sky is so big and blue as if
someone up there said
let me make this perfectly clear

MR. SNUFFLEUPAGUS

My first experience in queer art
was Mr. Snuffleupagus
a figment of the imagination
that existed first
in the mind of someone else
then was brought to Earth
I'm sitting by a book of *48 Preludes*
and Fugues vol. 1
by Johann Sebastian Bach
Extremes are a necessary element
to lasting art
and the word fugue is perfect
with a fugue you
have a contrapuntal composition
the short melody
and the loss of awareness
of my own identity
I leave my body when writing
return when my hands are cold
legs asleep
circulation needs to flow
to my brain and organs
but I really do and don't care
artists too can enjoy the exosphere

EARTH

A body of water is the mirror
of the natural world
and Earth is the first bathhouse
All the light is trapped under clouds today
like the underside of sheep
Please don't write this off as a stoner poem
I'm way more than high
want to cry in the same places
as Frank O'Hara for the simulacra
currently in a doozy
of a mid-life
crisis and got myself a moth tattoo
on a section of my tender misloved body
in blue yellow red
I leave my body for a full three hours
afterwards drank a birthday cake shot
that curdled like semen
slept with a man in total darkness
Above his bed a sign *Posivibes*
in glittering letters purple
tried to find his face in a pin of light
of his charging Apple computer and fell
in love with whom he was hiding from
have to save myself affection
afterwards removing the Second Skin
performing aftercare in the act of washing
my arm of plasma and goop
I can take better care of myself
On dating apps I'm less than
ten feet from the person I'm
intended to love

VESSEL

Art needs a vessel
Once I thought to save my voice
Instagram message was in vanishing mode
after a deep and vivid dream also a memory
of This Ain't the Rosedale Library
I had wandered my first year in Toronto
to find an art show with
people on their knees
balancing silver spoons on their noses
like there was something askew with the gravity
of the room which felt so still
and confident in the silence and balances
I never understood the significance
and grew up believing deer were herbivores
then I saw one chew to death a rodent
on the internet on Instagram
and I am trying to alter my algorithm
and in doing so find myself opening up

TURTLE

I travel a lot in my mind
it is the easiest way to leave the body
without the deprivation
tank price
I've found a place I like
inside the neck hole of my black hoodie
and tend to communicate
with little clicks from a
retractable pen
accidentally cut-and-paste two poems
is the easiest way to leave the Earth
be in a limbo of two worlds
My partner once knocked on my Earth
asked if I wanted to drive to Hamilton
I stared out the neck hole
there are days where the craving
when the desire is not to be perceived
of course it's okay
Having no sense of structure also
not a bad thing
People on Earth are still struggling
with the effects of postmodernism
Living alone I don't speak for days
then coaxed out to the park by a friend
not seen in eons
They went to Iceland and cleaned
the ocean of nets and tires and once a Barbie head
shared a hot tub with Björk
Their skin cells swam with her skin cells
and gave to me on the lips
of Riverdale Park East unnatural green flowers
they found in Toronto
I need the motivation to apply myself
for an artist grant at least

Not jealous on the subway I transfer
my entire self to a little turquoise bench
which is not an anchor but a place
on Google Maps and a calm colour
At Bathurst Station a mandible of pomegranate
becomes the myth the art the legend
My work is observational
A kind of captivity I have to sit in

CRAB

It would be nice to be
hypnotized by my dreams
Dreams where I read to you
a poem in my crab voice
a sonnet in a collection bought while tipsy
from the non-existent Eliot's Bookshop
the words simple bubbles first
maxilliped to third maxilliped
My email provider just asked me to verify
that I'm human completely
something not easily done
for as a queer it can take a lot
to convince the people in power
I have the same organs and teeth
and even I'm conflicted
As I have been raising myself up
under the purple glow of the Amazon
grow lights not unlike the fawn
from *Alice Through the Looking-
Glass* where there is a patient wait
for my new body and for the new monstera
leaf to unravel
But who knows anymore
you can get so close to something
and no longer see it

DONKEY-POWERED OPTIMISM

All the new spider egg sacs
in my kitchen window
are like a small newly discovered
solar system
I noticed them after removing myself
my two back molars
So intensely freeing the relief
My friend said I should see a doctor
with real pathos
Every morning after work at 3 a.m.
the taxi passes a statue of the donkey
with two broken legs
it is enough medicine
what the statue of this donkey means
to art
So what if some of the body disappears
during my lifetime
The statue was made to speak and push
back against statues of historical men
on strong horses seen everywhere
upholding their versions of a past
Ulysses gets what he deserves
having bored us to tears with epic
stories which of course are fabrications
and through the donkey statue
weakness is celebrated
In Mallo café I write in my notebook
in terms of the world I wonder
what something else would look like entirely
Through the window a woman stares
into the distance
slowly chewing a cucumber salad

REALITY

With my three water placements in astrology
I am told by an old science that I am
passionate about life
Living on this planet seems unwise
my friend told me over Old-Fashioneds
in a bar lit solely with candles
comforting is the eulogic light
Betelgeuse went supernova
We just have not experienced the aftermath
When I go home I google *eye*
sockets classified as depressions
It's difficult to live so long
and not feel a distant dying star
and what is the word for that
feeling where you leave the apartment
and do not know where to head
so you stand there wishing for invisibility
for celebrity news to find its way
out of your life
So tired of these glimpses into that realm
and mirror of the grotesque rich
people seem to emulate
On the subway I rise from my turquoise seat
Eavesdropping on two girls heading east
I think *these two need to get their friend some help*
The worry in their voices just
to discover their concern was intimate
info about a Los Angeles TV family
that will now be a permanent part
of knowledge that defines the contemporary
world for some unforeseen reason

THREE OF SWORDS

Or the decision at 3 a.m.
when birds are still
silhouettes on the power line
the sky a moot purple
above the Art of Emotions
Fine Art Gallery
the black wet sheen of night
and having passed the donkey statue
at Bay and St. Joseph
the instinct and desire not to use
Times New Roman tonight
It is just something I really really really
don't want to use again
and think *what are these other Matthews doing*
when I wake up at a man's house
After a flat rum and Coke and red Marlboro
using Times New Roman I wake
to the Vaderish whisper of his CPAP machine
its good to know he cares about dreams
I contain impulsive tendencies
Like amassing a collection of thirty-one plants
in a short euphoric time span
but I could not bring myself
to be alone tonight and when I close
my eyes into my own black
sheets I remember my friend who said *build*
yourself up out of nowhere
It's like a strength you summon to say no

JOKE

A man came into the bar
to sell me a face and body razor
Maybe I did not have these
the face and body
so important to gay culture
and identity I thought
playing the role of a Bacchanalian figure
from the myths
perhaps based on a real-life person
I stand in the darkness of my bedroom at 3 a.m.
existence seems likely
and is confirmed by my face
imprint on the pillow
Yes I love this visual confirmation
and have become obsessed with the night
and the works of Jean Rhys
which I bury myself in and read
on the turquoise bench
waiting for a connection on the Yonge Line
A person in plaid was reading
Voyage in the Dark
something lit up inside me
when they asked *What book*
without a question mark looking at the hands
in front of me like a baby
I say *Good Morning, Midnight*
He says *book sounds English*
To be precise I say *Wales not whales*
What is one letter you never say in Wales?
He jokes rising from his seat
but all I can imagine is a big blue fin
cutting through the blue ocean
A vowel he said and *good night*
I was lost and left
thinking in *whale language*

GHOST

Once inside a beer fridge in Halifax
which had once been a mortuary cooler
I turned a corner past the Labatt Blue
through a dank watery metallic smell
and walked through a ghost in full tuxedo
a remnant of the *Titanic* sinking
I would love to know where people are coming from
if this form of energy still in formal wear
masturbated at least twice a day
as a news anchor once suggested and when I come
home after last call I forget about self-romance
and google how to figure out in Word
how to stop the first word
on the next line from turning into a capital
and end the night cleaning my computer screen
of skin flakes and other losses

THE ARTISTS

I'm always mesmerized by graffiti art
and the artists themselves
who are never seen but leave their publicity
like they live in an invisible world
none of whom I am sure about
if they are in my real life or a periphery
At Bathurst and Bloor above the Jerk King
someone sprayed the phrase *Cloud Glare*
I am amazed and impressed by the placement
how the letters technically had to be written
upside down while so high up cloudlike
and myself unable to lose my cloud voice
due to a study I participated in
poetic symbology
Once very late at night I jumped
off the Bathurst streetcar near the ravine
the impulse surprised me
when a man in red silently ran up
and blew in my ear
when I turned
he was paces behind me
I didn't know I could let someone so close
It was a man I noticed on the streetcar with me
while listening to Björk's "Jóga" in my headphones
maybe he did it to be intimate
with me and he followed me for a few blocks
I was not thinking about my friend
or Iceland but why my ear
why this location and that placement
why did he select me
as his own specific vessel

RESURRECTION

At work a man walked in little circles
outside the bathroom
I went over
asked if he was okay
without looking up from his phone
he said *too many men*
crucifix tattoo on his head
Easter weekend
I nodded and said *I know*
Just when you think they are gone
they rise

UNRULY SONNET

Hard to love yourself faced with uncertainty
the reciprocation of love
could be returned
I tried to put a version of Lacan
from the mirror into a poem
he escaped the sonnet built for him
subjects of neuron dream and suspension
and I called my friend on Instagram
to show him my gemstones
protective crystals
despite the night previous
when I couldn't find the way out
of the bedroom and ran
my hands down the walls
using my fingers as legitimate eyes
looking for the doorknob
as if I was the security personnel
patting someone down before
they fly away

CLOUD GRAPE

On the bridge near Sorauren Park
there are two silhouettes
handing out grey felt hearts and hugs
which I decline due to syntax error
moon waning gibbous and maybe dreams
are a kind of bioluminescence
brief manifestations in our dreamy skulls
the organ that is also a visual artist
Please take me to your darkest field
lay me in the grass to say hello to Galileo
Orion Cassiopeia and the Swan
they have been up there so long
and you have been so good to me
though your theory of why we blush
because it is a biological trait
left over from our lizard ancestor
sounds like a dark-web conspiracy
In the park a woman is counting
the rings of a tree
I want to lean in to make an inquiry
how long was it married to the Earth
In Greenfield Grocery
the hallucinogenic cleaning aisles
on this street and then all the cleaning aisles
in my neighbourhood and further out
the city and pink blue yellows
and my friend cleaning the oceans
of Iceland and now there was a dream
about you and me where I was Hermia
extracting myself from every system
that was damaging
I walked through a spider's web
fell over my face like a veil
while I pedalled down King Street

distracted by a garbage bin proclaiming
break down your boxes I mean Cixous
has been doing that since the sixties
but you haven't read *Dream I Tell You*
In Montréal a man suggested to me therapy
in terms of sleep for my snoring
could rip the very fabric of night
It could be a heart condition he warned
as his heart was diagnosed
for his troubled sleeping was a sign
I asked him *then why are my dreams so real*
then held him up outside Coop Le Cagibi
the soup was squash that day
and told him that I felt real
heat twice in a dream it was April
with snowdrops in a parkette near my apartment
I walked at 3 a.m. from my job
past Eyesore Cinema in the glow of night
a man on a ladder throwing fedoras out
a second-floor window into a dumpster
which proclaimed not a single word
I stood watching him from below
high above me this man on a ladder
throwing fedora after fedora into the night
He climbed down and touched my hand
in a sincere way his hands were hot
to the touch and asked me what I needed
In my apartment a carnelian-red blister
formed on the back of my hand
I pulled out leaves wet with my body
fluid and hot as my body with actual heat
I clean it under the sink and squeeze
out tinier leaves which felt like a balm
and the nerve of that guy thinking
I needed anything at all

PLANETARIUM

I learned about the universe
inside a silver mobile planetarium
Zero knowledge of constellations or Zeus
or systems the signifier of pomegranate
introduction to the milky way
my first memory of darkness
it felt like I wasn't present in body
sitting in a circle with others I knew
would be there in the light
where above us my first simulation
in the form of galaxies and the Earth's
rotation this was before knowledge
of stars as a noun
the idea of myth and academic traditions
in the study of the subconscious
how beautiful stars could be
how reliable and constant and full of gas
and plasma as my biology
and at 3 a.m. tonight I can view Neptune
and simply exist in a universe
read of its diamond rains
I admire how distant was this event
how untouchable
as an adult learning I too can appear
a million light years away

DRIVING BY THE DONKEY STATUE

I exist somewhere between the delivery
of chicken fingers and the taxi home
If I have to live
to serve I will refer to hard liquor as spirits
I'm such a struggle bus
when it comes to quitting drinking
the supernatural implications
When in the dark of my bedroom
things come to me from the subconscious
my zero knowledge of Plato
and the other master thinkers
On the subway a woman is screaming
about loving the connective tissues
I don't speak up enough
A majority of my formal education
was meant to maintain the historic
lies and it would be nice to reset
my brain with the end of a safety pin
I say *I wish I was dead* then read
a poem written by Dorothea Lasky
that makes longing hurt very good
with her signature depth
like the time I saw her in real life
at Public Pool in Los Angeles
I think this is the epiphany
That I both fear and crave
the factory reset

LOS ANGELES SEQUENCE

I see my favorite stranger drinking
Coca-Cola from a wineglass
Maybe also the view of potential future self
two days before flying to California
to eat salted fruit in a swan-shaped boat in Echo Park
His computer is one of the first editions
of the Apple laptop and he announces
that he is *open to love for his life is very slow*
raises his wineglass and falls asleep
in front of the PowerBook
From the sky I imagine California a long
black cocktail dress the night lights
amethyst and citrine against the arm
muscle of the sea and my boyfriend
bought me an Our Lady of Guadalupe candle
in the likeness of Amy Winehouse
I lit it every night to be
the one who blew it out
watching the single flame dance
to wonder why I ruined the day
by spelling out *death* in the sands of Malibu
despite the world being new to me
the scenery around so weirdly blue
In this world mountains sat like toads
against this pink-orange sky
You're in the parking lot with a Parliament
from Canada hanging from your lip
pointing to me and the mountain *Big Bear*
and dusk is pink and blue
the light slides over the land
like somewhere some potential god
is peeking in after opening the lid on Tupperware
the moon faint and holographic
Palm Springs felt so temporary

to me I suppose it was ephemeral
the moon was beautiful but left
I wanted to try acting and pretend to fit in
eating an avocado straight from the skin
instead I order a Miller Half-Life
after the eight-course meal that faced the road
later we moved our bodies together
on the heart-shaped bed while
a pay-per-view movie ended
in the corner and I am okay
with the scenery
driving through the rock and forms
felt like Saskatchewan to me
though you do not agree so I don't know
who I am between these mountains
as you puff your cigarette out the window
of our rental car
sun on your face like a puppy
We stop at the giant orange for novelty
ended up inside the Cathedral
City 7-Eleven where I kissed Pepsi from your lips
went a little further
your hand on my thigh
through the sleepy eternal mountains

SOBRIETY FOR ME IS LIKE SAN FRANCISCO

A place I've never been
in my entire life is San Francisco
I don't think I am going to make it
At a reading in Vancouver Weldon Kees
was the poet I performed for the Dead
Poets Reading Series
It had been a delight to
in my voice
read in his voice
the audience left for a bar
near my old house at First and Commercial
Where I could look in the outline of clouds
up in the dark grapey night
Once I tried to make love in a mirror
and it was a study
of how to mimic being loved
I laugh at this skit I will never write
where a character is surprised they got into heaven
somehow their ex finds out and says
god I might not be able to go he might be there
I'd really like one day
to see San Francisco and cross over
the Golden Gate Bridge and see the sites of
the gay-rights movement
I also love fog
In San Francisco I'd treat myself right
order the Dungeness crab
despite my hatred for the creatures
everything deserves a chance
And I don't know how long I could even stay
though a majority of the city is on the sea
where I have always been
fine with the magnetic pull I feel
between moon and water

even though I can't
begin to comprehend the long relationship
I'd just like to go to San Francisco
and walk up the really big hill just once

LOW VALLEY AND BARE LANDS

In town a man said *we won't laugh*
if you use the ladies' room for the line
for men was long and I had a hole
in the pocket of my pink bomber
jacket but there was no shame
for the man that I personally felt
because in my other pocket green
beach glass tiny shells like baby teeth
collected from tide pools so blue
and the sky being a total mood
ring it just felt memorable too
because George Michael died
on the radio while we passed
the Huntington Beach Oil Field
and saw the tiny silver fish
just starting their life on Earth
and *some people are just careless*
with words I think to myself
driving down Highway 10
past the Radisson Park Inn
Los Angeles express lane ahead
I'm not thinking of the man
just Laguna Beach the blue water
and how it would fall at my feet
like tears I never celebrated

CLOUD GLARE

Have you ever astral projected writing a poem
I leave the body at least
there are moments my wet mysterious brain
has me believing
I have somehow been absent in life
and things are tense tonight so I am going to sit
back and relax and mind my business
and I tweeted *turn me into condos daddy*
My friend texted me immediately and stern
No emoji
OMG what happened?
I blame reality TV for the drama of his reaction
I had been looking at a new building development
that had been covered with ephemeral art
like a new skin
a soup can in the style of the Warhol
America's Condensed Stonewall Gay Love Riot
I texted *was trying to be humorous*
Maybe I make people worry
please don't
I will never be condos

SKELETON

I'm a very active person in the art
of destroying myself
but my skeleton is with me
in the form of shadow on a day with sun
Life's a shady business anyway
My computer is constantly asking me to prove
my identity
in terms of not AI
not robot or human simulation
It feels like the computer knows I am trying
to change my algorithm
I am just looking for a psychiatrist
to take my brain out
It's healthy to have something you want
to forget but that self-care gets you so far
On hold I draw a tear-shaped fish
with the words *blood test* and *layaway*
surrounding it with more tear shapes
while I listen to muzak
and the voice upstairs of my neighbour on hold
with Canada Revenue Agency
In the imagined waiting room
I tell people I am here for the recovery
of the Kemps ridley sea turtle
who I root for despite not being able
to understand their life
I don't mention artificial intelligence
sitting in a chair that does not exist
I just wonder if *are more things AI than not AI*
should be the new *to be or not to be*

BLUET

A book of poetry astonished me I forgot
it was a book not Instagram Messenger
as if the poet
was typing to me personally
I went home and ate a strawberry sundae
feeling my cynicism
about things that are asked of me to complete
and it leaves me
My friend said I was so naive
he saw me in a cult
and it felt like he was jealous of happiness
something created not by myself
but secretions and I am told serotonin
I don't want to be convinced
to doubt my own mind
That night I decide for myself to change
the position of my bed

GETTING GROCERIES

The woman in line does not want lasers
touching her vegetables
that cover the conveyor belt
in the most luxurious canopy of leaves
but the grocery code for mango works
no longer for anyone
so like myself the fruit is tired
I really should have chosen to make porn
for the bear community
when I had the opportunity in 2005
so just a reminder that choices are fine
going skinny-dipping in the Pacific at 3 a.m.
for instance or collecting your thoughts
in voice memos
I use my knowledge of scansion
on the drink cooler and come back
with a cold Ethos bottled water and
a desire for the ocean moon and tide

ADAGE

I miss the underwear of the people I loved
and realize on Harbord Street
my life has a long life
I have my headphones in listening
to the Cocteau Twins
Language is so destroying
The little televisions in the subway
Their persistent loom
They are there to scare me
remind me of Kim Kardashian
and her latest invention
the bra that makes nipples look hard
my train is about to come
on the turquoise bench at Bloor
how much can be real
At home I spit on a philodendron leaf
later it dries like plastic
on its little heart-shaped face

DARK CLOUD OVER MY TOWN

I leave the door open a slit
at the bathhouse
in my life there is appreciation
for surrealism
because the image of a man opening a door
for me not expecting a writer
to be sitting there working on edits
for the next book
I just need that energy in my life
to defy the expectation
computer paper tucked under my chin
with me in the room is one bottle
of blue Gatorade and a room key
on a red slinky
around my naked glenohumeral joint
and that is all I need
a clonazepam melting on my tongue
and a man walking in the blue shadows
holding an armful of towels
like he found a cloud
and must return it to somewhere

HAVISHAM

A psychologist describes desire
as *your blood*
needing oxygen on Google
when I thought it meant *to long*
or *longing* or *to want*
Merriam-Webster cites
yearning as noun
but I have been in the dark
when there has just been me
and my heart beating

MOONSTONE

In a repair shop I kiss a mechanic
in front of several mirrors
inside True Centre Muffler and Care
and it is similar to therapy
All the versions of me go on forever
I like the image and how art is here
and the scent of oil
how things are fixed here
the smell of fresh red paint
in the otherwise grey room
I came here anonymously
but a person on TikTok said
gazing at your form
can improve self-compassion
I am pondering in a Jane Austen
manner *is regret immune*
to ephemeralism I am briefly
here in several forms and distances
looking for someone
who may never be present

GOODBYE PSYCHIC OCTOPUS

It's uplifting to know we no longer need
Let go and let god there is a common
octopus with powers divine
I've never been sure of anything except one summer
I believed in an emerald
green frog living in my brain
for the brain itself resembled an egg sac
and everyone thought I was suffering
from mental illness
not for a second did anyone think
what a little poetic symbologist
I hold on to this idea like a moon
holds on to little wisps of darkness
I can't eat an animal who can open a jar
problem solve or dream
on independent brain activity
science states if dreams are occurring
they are like gifs or YouTube video clips
I just hate the feeling of anyone being
underestimated especially if my dreams are
so similar to their dreams

GATORADE

The upstairs neighbours are fucking
so hard I want to bring up a Gatorade
they seem into it and it is rhythmic
not like artificial intelligence at all
it is very human when they stop
and one asks *did I hurt you*
I am returning from a series of art
shows and became fixated on skin
particles eyelashes sweat tears or ear hair
have made it into the layers
of paint of the Blue Period
It is never discussed what we lose
in our art process or method
I drank wine in a churchyard
with the blue door off Queen Street
lost in thoughts of consecrated ground
when a cop with the audacity of Christ
took my bottle and poured the blood
on the cement trying to humiliate me
when I said my future was poetry
he asked *are you not sure of your future*
now and he was not full of love
and maybe unnecessary like the work
of Picasso and not full of passion
or tenderness like my upstairs neighbours
who cry out for different reasons above me

HOWL

My friend's dog Gary howls out
to an ambulance he can't see
and is demonstrating a compassion
I can hear it in his tone
I don't know what he believes
what the pitch and tone of the siren
is saying to him or telling him
for this is dog knowledge
something innate inside Gary
telling him to call out and lead
the ambulance to a safe den or blanket
it is an inspiration to me
I try to understand his dog brain
how it works after years of descending
from the grey wolf and his urgency
is about more concern and being told
he's a good person and reminds me
of the time I disappeared
in a shopping mall and it called my name
and I was returned to the Kmart
I wonder if someone is injured
the ambulance is living and hurt
Gary's howl will lead the vehicle to safety
and he stares out into the distance
with big grape eyes and I am not a scholar
of ancient dog memory but he is sure
something is wrong in the distance

SWAN DIVE

In the bathroom someone wrote
DREAM DICKS
in big stupid letters
maybe I took it the wrong way
but impulsively
there are few times I get to fight
back against the phallus
the phallocentric nature
of Earth itself
to have accomplished a goal
with a comma
DREAM, DICKS

THE EMBASSY

I had imprinted on this big fat Dell computer
full of my personal musings
one summer and took it drinking
woke up at the bottom of the stairs
surprised after having hit every stair
I was not broken
as I stood at the urinal could read
the archaic language of the bathroom
knowledge and the articulation
of time and existence
a capsule of human consciousness
DEEP HOMO
revere da deer
be present be reverent
so my vision is fine
love utopia and *cumbucket 3000*
I deleted my Twitter in red caps lock
My motherboard was destroyed
and a black-blue bruise eclipsed
my tender and pale ass
so I am a regular
human being after all iOS
I don't get any bone tests and dream
of tiny bones being reabsorbed
by my body because it is amazing

KAREN DALTON

I am finally being heard by devices
and must navigate settings
to increase my personal world
an online article said my phone
only does this because it wants to help
I have heard that order of words
in a sentence structure before
Please take me to the darkest field
to a Karen Dalton song where
the clear night and gravity support
this third supermoon of the year
giving us what scientists say is 90 percent
I'm told when I search *the night sky*
tonight from my location
I bought a turquoise Thermomix
from Amazon and feel seen as an apologist
of capitalism because the Jeff Bezos
New Shepard 4 rocket launch
by my Covid friend bubble
In Trinity Bellwoods on the lip of the dog
bowl which is a deep crater my friend
says *the sky is trans* and I say *pandemic*
brain to the sole cloud in the air
thinking *billionaire in the mesosphere*

GASLIGHT ME

I am a hypocrite whose first encounter
with panopticons was an egg sac
of the frog common to Nova Scotia
It's just not relaxing being perceived
the stress gives me eye floaties
I put on a cute outfit and feel stupid
and hear that some influencers
we perceive as being real humans
are truly artificial intelligence
and I can't tell if the cute animal account
is exposing me to misogynist language
and even sitting on the bus weirds me out
the 501 Queen car has bedbugs
In Trinity Bellwoods I saw a dog
walking on its hind legs and trying
to catch a moth in its mouth like a person
while I'm not insulted by this interpretation
being human isn't all it appears to be

ZARDULU

I'm trying to pay more
attention to my well-being
and my version of reality
things happen on the internet
which disprove some upheld beliefs
then discredit others but this
is exactly what the Libra emoji
is for everyone believed that Pizza Rat
was just a real unstaged rat
I'm listening to a podcast right
now that will change your mind on that
hope this is not coming off nonchalant
but I believe animals have goals
especially when I saw the sheep
with the bucket on her head like
there will be no follow-up questions
I read that when grass is cut or destroyed
that smell we all proclaim to love
is actually a distress call from a world
we can't even begin to imagine

COMMUNIST DAUGHTER

In an Ossington bar we listen
to the A-side then based on the merit
of whichever record we listen
to the B-side and that night a man
told me I had the eyes of Miriam Margolyes
only years ago they reminded a man
of the eye in *Un Chein Andalou*
I think this was a way for him to ease
into a Criterion film discussion I refused
to talk about anything except *Scorpio Rising*
by Kenneth Anger and nights prior
to the first man who spoke to me
I ate the garnish from his drink
I felt myself starving for something
I decided to move away from a friend
who described herself as Stalin's Homegirl
I said *didn't he murder like millions*
of people but I was very incorrect and
I wanted to live with freedom and not live
like a living thing learning to trust again

FRANK O'HARA

The ways in which outside influences
invade the personal life disturb me
am I supposed to believe tear ducts
an essential part of the male body
are becoming useless due to evolution
I can't worry if everyone is flushing
their medication down toilets
which may end up in the water supply
because I'm being made to pay and live
on Earth not a direct quote just
something I argued on speakerphone
when my friend tried to estimate the total
bottles of lube in the Great Pacific Garbage
Patch and when I emerge at St. George
Station the moon is an empty plate
And I see a rat drag a Styrofoam
container into an alley and I'm amazed
at their energy after such a long day

CLOTHO

Opened my eyes to see a spider
on the wall the day I overslept
for a co-worker's celebration of life
and I clipped my nails into the sink
remembering when he fixed the pressure
on the vegetable sprayer in the produce section
when people were insane for celery water
outside I passed a man
with dandelion puffballs in his hair
pink Nike High Tops on his feet
I walked around the block
just for a little sunshine and air
something Earth does without ceremony
in my absence the spider manoeuvered
across my bedroom on what was like
zero tether or some invisible silk
human eyes aren't meant to understand
or see all threads and connections

DO NOT TOUCH THE NOTEBOOKS

I don't let men get too close to me
close up they will see my secret mysteries
I am growing out my silky black hairs
of my nose in hope men develop
an aversion to me
During the Olympics I wouldn't go
down on a man who promised to burn me
into the Great Canadian Literary Landscape
the flowery language was enough
and this was a favour to me
I have not won any medals for sucking dick
Men tell me *such beautiful eyes* so I won't leave
one foot on his bedroom floor
while the openly gay diver from Laval
claimed silver in the 3-metre springboard
I tell men to *text me to let me know*
to text you and pray no one responds
I need to figure my beard as mine is a face
hider and I want to be luscious for me
and I like to leave my shirt on during sex
because I have a scar a man once licked
that transported me back to the emergency room
only in terms of scars and memory
and the complex prison system of the brain
He asked why all my notebooks were empty
I said *I wrote* and *please do not touch*
the notebooks I'm growing them out

SHELTER

In the forest I had come
across a deer skeleton
and there is silence when
you walk up to a death
I have to take in that this animal
probably did what it could
Earlier I had swallowed a whole
moth that fell through the mouth
of my beer can and it was a looper
moth as there were infestations
during that year of life
Alone looking at the moon
in my cliché era I remember
stuttering to articulate in words
what my eyes in the world
would see but this skeleton
was the whole sentence
the stages of death are articulated
so quiet and quiet
the medical system is crumbling
I had taken the skull to my boyfriend
who was disgusted with me
so want me to dig
up something I find scary
there is a percentage of me
writing a poem to keep my mind
off the addiction of opening up
a beer and entering
the black dreamless world
writing just to leave my body
because I'm very sick of my own skeleton
the noun that peeks when I smile
I don't use words to create excuses
that hurts my feelings

when he says *sounds like you*
are making excuses
when what I do is try
explaining a verb for my own heart
to think humans created language
but I can't speak to him
It's strange to think of fields
dedicated to skeletons
I want to be fed to a tree
when released of this Matthew body
so some part of me can be
a shelter for the living
thing staggering from the highway

BODY

I was caught in the search history
of the family computer downloading
homosexual content typing *gay sex*
in the browser to see a body
download on the slow dial-up
from a telephone wire
a cowboy naked in a green field
moving in a loop like a gif
and what was known about lust
I learned from the encyclopedia
had not heard of an endorphin
knew Eros was dangerous
but the people from Greek myth
were bisexual and transformed
lovers into animals as a form
of punishment and ate grapes
which are so expensive now
I was meant to feel embarrassed
by the surveillance and betrayal
of the computer but I am far
My friend says they never asked to be
here paying to live on Earth
not to live how they want
well I'm living on Bathurst Street
staring at the ceiling not focusing
on the pressure to perform
the right idea of the male gender
and being terrified of having a body
that was not mine

ELLIPSES

I was told that my body was not human
It succeeded in defying a classification
system which does not concern me
I have an abductor muscle which fails
occasionally due to mechanical error
and once a man twisted my nipples
so hard like they were a car ignition
and maybe pornography ruined me
for its interpretation and use of intimacy
in its artistic approach to mimesis
but I managed to survive adolescence
reading the immense classic novels
from 1800s England originally serialized
in newspapers after being outed
by the internet service technician
and the world is judgemental sure
and sitting in the bathtub in the dark
listening to the onomatopoeia of water
doing my own system upgrade to identify
and isolate any sort of internal error

ESC

The main flaw perceived in myself
is how I'm scared to live
unsure how to process this inarticulate
trauma and have it treated seriously
I think a strength is the use of escapism
through books and my extensive internal world
where I am not deeply hurt
by what I had become
and done to myself
I recollect fishing rainbow trout
on Kidney Lake
with an unidentified male relative
who I had to stand a certain way
for the in public world
and I realized in my life I would
disappoint a number of people
but either way the fish comes
like up from a dream
mouthing words with *O* vowels
I would unhook the fish
and look into its golden eyes
shaped like little tears
a part of the vast ocean
the fish lay on its side
in a white bucket
trying to catch itself a breath
searching for the words
its mouth open and buffering
silent and mental dial-up

SERVING FACE

Used to stare at the ceiling
of the living room
and see faces in the stucco
it was like studying an art
that was older than your time on Earth
it is a condition called *pareidolia*
the want to see meaning
in random objects
Normalize seeing things
that are not there
surprised face of the electrical outlet
is the most common
and once considered seeing faces
a symptom of psychosis
and is now a normal part
of the human experience
like computer vision
the idea of the grocery store
or the cloud I witnessed morph
from my face to your face

DIAL-UP

I had a hard time growing up into a boy
and did not succeed in this goal
had no managerial skills of which to speak
having grown to fear the cubicle
In the bathtub I'd tuck my genitals between
my thighs and float
high in clouds of a whole bottle
of wildflower shampoo
until the water would answer
who I would be by turning cold
I would sit by the ocean
before ASMR became chic
and from a 1991 encyclopedia learned sciences
of tidal pulls moon tides
the solitary moon pushing the ocean
me towards it
I think of the Deborah Cox lyric
looking to the moon I whisper *just be good to me*
my first orgasm
a right arm arched over a body
new bridge
warm water then moonstone
the Illinoisan who claimed he came
from another world
the first to ask *tell me about you*
I was fifteen and he was forty-six years older
called me *Bluenoser* over the physical
and heavy rotary telephone
I felt understood and well described
but out of the depth in a personal awareness
I was conditioned to fear

SOFT CORE

It's hard to admit to myself
that I have a life
in this body
I feel my life is long enough
and I can't imagine anything else
now that I am the new person
at a minimum wage job
I drank to create my own cinema
and pass the CINEFORUM sign
on Bathurst and I have a black screen
in my head
to remember not one dream
my brain a powered-down Toshiba television
I wish I could have let it be known
that I was queer earlier in my memory
without the years of anguish
and duplicity but I learned to act
a real life and watched news reports
about the HIV/AIDS crisis
blood contamination
like the media was trying conversion
therapy over the air waves
It would have been way cooler
than what we ended up doing
and I reminisce about the queer art
the world could have experienced
I came out and acted as gay as possible
based on Hollywood depictions of queerness
films about straight people coming to terms
with homosexuals or gays succumbing to AIDS
I remember hiding who I was I
used to think that there was no gay cinema
until a soft-core porn titled *Boyfriends*
on channel 500 and felt this

kaleidoscope of repressed emotion
enough for everyone
It was looking through an eyehole
at a desire that troubled my body
when the only thing is I'm living

IAMB

I have made it hard to see myself
as anything other than a fat depressed person
who just wants to recover
that is just unfair to the people around me
Acceptance is tough
but I'm not taking a moral inventory
of myself
I wore purple and my friend called me
Grimace from the Kingdom of McDonald's
on Google Chat
how can you do that to someone
with no sense of self
This kind of language takes me
to a new height in body dysmorphia
where I'm comfortable telling my joke
What is the loneliest thing on Earth?

ZOOM

I found my people much later in life
I can make better choices like staying home
to watch *Breathless* by Jean-Luc Godard
on my friend's Criterion account
I am much better over text or email
I used to go to parties
beg my straight friends not to mention
my quiet gay homosexual life
worried about fielding questions
about the lifestyle or people
offering services where I can seek help
and of course solace
I interrupted them to tell a story
about the time I was giving lazy head
to my friend for like an hour
and then he looked down at me
and said *when did you get here?*
then forced out a long uncomfortable
laughter and it eliminated the half jokes
of taking someone's boyfriend
into the small room with the deep-freeze
but did not convince men
I was not into them sexually
and at that point would have blown
everyone at the Christmas party
to eat some cheeseballs in peace
why I'm not more flamboyant
I don't have the answer for that
and ask if they are hinting around
to gain trade secrets enjoying great anal
what I'm saying is I would have
loved to have stayed but this Christmas
party could have been an email

DESIRE

I met a man who called me *lover*
over the internet
and worked in metallurgy
a real blacksmith who reminded me
of Hephaestus
He fed deer that lived on the land
with his bare hand
In the evening I would read upstairs
in the sweetheart window
The Moonstone by Wilkie Collins
And he would hammer metal
creating something in his mind
and bringing out here into the world
I loved the brutality
later he would come lay his cock
down the spine of my book
not from a position of power
but to say *yes*
the delivery was hilarious and sexy
because he wanted me
head down and I loved to hide
inside my brain during sex
like the internet I open up
window after window after window
to not feel the glass and relax
when he called me his salt lick
I gestured non-verbally and drank
non-verbally on the balcony
soaked in pheromones
little white summer moths
catching moonlight while he ate
an apple off the knife

PEA CLOUD

My father used to tell me to *go*
get your own personality
lose weight but I never had money
felt empty handed
I would sit in the living room
reading *Funk and Wagnalls*
a bound set of exclusive encyclopedias
myths of Greek gods and facts of topography
In the paragraph on Aphrodite
I felt an affinity to rise from the ocean
feeling like I was born
made of seafoam cloud
I acted like her
after my own father was forced
into vasectomy
at the hands of my mother
realizing there would be no other like me
no social currency was I to need
With my sun in Cancer
I had what the sea gave me
a shell in which to retreat
while my father iced his testicles
with frozen peas
I left him there on ice
my moon glow in Scorpio
In Toronto I was told on two occasions
that my aura is blue
with red and little black dots
like Morse code
I had difficulty communicating
in words and alphabet
but if my body was dot dot dot
it was punctuation
ellipses

When I witness two humans embrace
I see the ampersand
Days after I finish a book I find it hard
to return to myself
I spent years as Miss Havisham
I want to be this person made up
of someone else
My horoscope or phone guides me
so if my text auto-corrects *I think*
I am working through Mon–Thurs
to *I am ethereal* how can I argue

SALAMANDER

I realized humans possessed the ability to heal
when I first cut myself
along the medial longitudinal arch
hunting a leopard
frog that floated in a pond
on a rock shaped like a shark
tooth and I feel like I absorbed some
frog power as it was me predictably
hopping to the safety
of the car while imagining the creatures enjoying
my blood and concerned the blood
would not know to stop
I loved the animal world I was happy
in a rock pile lifting stones like Atlas
to see the creatures react to the
addition of light to their world
a salamander who preferred her world
of secrecy waterways and cool soil
I loved it when it rained in summer
worms became the grass of night
creatures who could fuck themselves
My first ex was a painter
so dedicated to his work that he pissed
in water bottles
so not to break his concentration
but it was not great for the Earth
he was a queer artist and his basement smelled
of wet soil and fall leaves
our first date was a forest walk like the Cure
song I was not aware of the need
I had for more gay content
like why couldn't it have always been like this
a homosexually fuelled life
It surprises me my power

how much I have had to keep straight
it is nice to enjoy yourself
in the bathhouse Jacuzzi
with a room of your own
your head a poetic figure

EX MOON MIST

Waking up from a dream
where you are getting head
from your boyfriend giving you real head
with moonlight on his face
wrapped in the smell of boy sweat
the sky yellow and pink
a time of day reminding me
of Moon Mist ice cream
the colour inspired by transitions
late afternoon to early evening
when bats came out of a crabapple
tree to eat moth and June bug
the light drinkers of any light
I hated to come out in early morning
being more of a darkness person
my room also had been so dark
but to watch this baby blue then pink
seep out from what was the pupil
of the sky over Lake Ontario
it's amazing that all this happens
because we are all stuck in the Earth loop
Now I understand that salamander
her reaction to a rock being lifted
perhaps for her a first sunrise and here
my whole life being lit up
my own eyes opening like a blind

NOTES AND ADDITIONS

I just wanted to thank Sheryda Warrener
who is simply one in a million
when it comes to working
with writers and encouraging them
to push themselves I learned so much
from the books and writing she
recommended when I was deeply
writing and thinking about
this book and during the editing
process of *Terrarium*
I also need to thank Jim Johnstone
for publishing some of these poems
in the chapbook *ICQ* (Anstruther Press)
Thank you to the people who appear
in these poems and to other writers
like KC MF CM RT x 2 ML HN and others
I honestly didn't know if I could finish
the book and I am so thankful to the people
at Goose Lane and the editors that worked
on the book with me, Alan and Martin
very eternally grateful to you both.
Special thanks to Justina for her cool visions,
Sacha, Torch in Sky, Romy, and to Gary
for allowing me to see beyond myself

The poem "Bluets" references Maggie Nelson's collection of the same name.

The poem title "Dark Cloud over My Town" is taken from a Robyn song, "Dancing On My Own" (2010).

The poem "Head" borrows the line "let me make this perfectly clear" from Gwendolyn MacEwan's poem of that name in *Afterworlds* (1987).

The poem "Joke" mentions the work of Jean Rhys.

The donkey statue mentioned in this collection was created by artist Myfanwy MacLeod. The work, *Primrose* (2019), is based on an actual baby donkey who was born prematurely in 2012 at the Bind Equine Veterinary Practice in Shropshire, England.

Edited by Sheryda Warrener.
Cover and page design by Julie Scriver.
Cover image: Justina Dollard, *Dream Image*, 2017. Collection of the artist. @theladyjustina on Instagram.
Printed in Canada by Coach House Printing.
10 9 8 7 6 5 4 3 2 1

Library and Archives Canada Cataloguing in Publication

Title: Terrarium / Matthew Walsh.
Names: Walsh, Matthew, 1982- author.
Description: Poems.
Identifiers: Canadiana 20230533728 | ISBN 9781773103327 (softcover)
Subjects: LCGFT: Poetry.
Classification: LCC PS8645.A4747 T47 2024 | DDC C811/.6—dc23

Goose Lane Editions acknowledges the generous support of the Government of Canada, the Canada Council for the Arts, and the Government of New Brunswick.

Goose Lane Editions is located on the unceded territory of the Wəlastəkwiyik whose ancestors along with the Mi'kmaq and Peskotomuhkati Nations signed Peace and Friendship Treaties with the British Crown in the 1700s.

Goose Lane Editions
500 Beaverbrook Court, Suite 330
Fredericton, New Brunswick
CANADA E3B 5X4
gooselane.com

Known for a "compelling, original voice" (*Canadian Literature*), Matthew Walsh grew up in Nova Scotia and now lives in Toronto. Walsh's poetry has been published in *Joyland*, the *Capra Review*, the *Malahat Review*, and *Geist*. Walsh is also the author of the chapbook *ICQ* and the celebrated debut *These are not the potatoes of my youth*, a finalist for both the Trillium Book Award and the Gerald Lampert Memorial Award.

Photo: David Schoonover, @forestwindspine